PRIMAVERA

A COLLECTION OF POETRY

EDITOR: ADITI GHOSH

Made with ♥ on the Notion Press Platform
www.notionpress.com

I dedicate this book to the students' fraternity of Maryam ajmal Women's College of Science & Technology, Hojai. It compiles the collection of poems self-composed by the students and teachers while inaugurating hand made magazine for the Department of English.Hence, to preserve the poems, this step served as a blessing.I hope this publication will inspire them to elevate their creativity and expression as well developing the Writing skill

Contents

Foreword

This book will serve as mirror to Self, realizing the collective skill of writers and an observation and self-assessment towards the creativity, imagination, critical sights.

Preface

"Express to express" find it's best expression through words in the form of Poetry. In the words of Keats, "If poetry does not come as naturally as the leaves to a tree, it had better not come at all". Creativity and Imagination led to the critical insights of the writers through their creation of expressions. This Book consists of a collection of poems self-composed by Women (teachers and Degree students) of Department of English, Maryam Ajmal Women's College of Science & Technology, Hojai (Assam). This poetry collection is a part of handmade magazine inaugurated by the Department in April,2021. The poems are the expressing different expressions celebrating the essence of creative imagination and power.

As an instructor to the students of Maryam Ajmal Women's College of Science & Technology, Hojai, I have tried my possible ways to retain and preserve the creativity and expression of the myriad voices through this book. I hope this will cater to the inspiration for more creativity, voices and expression.

Acknowledgements

I express my thanking gratitude to respective students and teachers of the Department of English, Maryam Ajmal Women's College of Science and Technology, Hojai for contrtibuting with their self-composed poems.

I also thank Latifa Begum, Nazhat Sultana, Nasrin Akhtar, Nondini Devi, Chamely Begum for forwarding me their sincere help.

I am grateful to my parents for their unconditional support. I am truly blessed to be a part of this family. I am also thankful to the members of my family, well-wishers, friends, seniors, and colleagues who have dedicated their time in helping me during the course of this study.

I express my thanking gratitude to the publishing house for your kind support.

Prologue

PROLOGUE

The flow of words into the waves of water

1. A New Beginning

All dark and gloomy, I was all night;
Night of misery and suffering
Nights of terror and fear.
Streets filled with sad cries and death faces.
It was all broken, fallen as the fallen angles.
Once beautiful once glorious,
They remember the past and cry at their sad plight.
They remember the days of happy faces and eyes
They remember the days of love and prosperity
once blossomed, once beautiful, once loved
Now crushed, fallen and forgotten
Trees of love and hope are now fare,
faded, lost as the lost years of youth.
from the dungeon of suffering
from the dungeon of misery
from the dark gloomy Night,
It will rise
To witness the birth of a new world
As after a lone dark night,
There is a beautiful sunlight, A dark break of wonder.
A light that sings even when the night is dark
Breaking the chain of curse, it'll divine.
Sweeping the dark, it'll shine.

Wiping the tears, it'll smile.
The world will be filled with happy leaves,
blossomed flowers, happy huts.
The dead faces will spread light and,
Again, there will be blossomed flower,
green leaves, happy huts.
The crushed bodies, crushed lives
will rise Again.
Again, there will be a beautiful world
Again, there will be a new beginning.
(By Ruhana Firdous)

2. I Am

Sometimes, I think,
I am not a poet
But I do express
The emotions in tranquillity
Sometimes, I think,
I am a poet
Yet, I am unable to express
the dictions of my emotional trace
I last myself in the conjunctive world
of thoughts, expression and imagination
I find reality in fantasy
and fantasy in reality
My emotions are high in serenity
and the words achieve its sublimity!
I find peace in the betweenness of my conscience;
Because I am an absent presence
And I am free to commence
the existence having no sense
I find myself singing the song of fallen leaves standing
amidst,
The hazardous landscape of industries
Also, fantasize myself embracing the things falling apart
Because I see a vision of art

Where the things gradually fall in part!
My words might be a chaos to you,
having some gibberish sense of name
Yet, I rejoice this expression of literariness
Where a meaning can also have a meaninglessness!
If you replicate my lines with a cram
You will familiarize yourself in Rene Descartes' Words -
"I think, therefore I am"
(By Aditi Ghosh)

3. The Song of Emotion

Lots of months and lots of fears have passed
Still the sound of wind and bees buzzed
Excitement of every summer, spring and winter
with a soft inland murmur.
Those beautiful days of wonder
How one forgets but always remember.
Those rays of Sun at morning and evening
which seems every day is a new beginning.
(By Taiyeba Kawsar)

4. Shame? / An Honor

Walking by the night
Towards the benighted light,
Unknown of the fact of
She being judge.
She, so powerful in emotions,
So brave in conviction
Is losing all of herself
In the hands of cruelty
I am an honour, says she,
To the pointing world.
I'm a miss, says she
To the ones busy throwing stones on
her way.
Walking by the night
She's reminded of
the arrows thrown
Upon her life the
Moment her body
Felt her soul,
The moment of her mother
Hiding behind the walls
Protecting her from the dread.
Thrive I, says she, reigning

Over the obstacles
For her words enliven
My inner power
For to conquer me
Own space and
Walking by the night
I hold the power to fight.
(By Shyma Begum)

5. Me To Myself

Me, All Alone
Within the four walls
Tried a thousand times to find myself.
Looking at the birds, the insects
And a wide-open field
And then to myself,
Sometimes behind the curtains of the door.
I, listen to the gossips
For what is happening outside the four walls,
Me, when all alone
The person I miss the most is my mother,
Miss the moments we spend together.
Yes, I tried a thousand times to find Myself.
(By Nazhat Sultana)

6. She

She is not just a mother, she is life giver

She is smart, strong, emotion

She is action, passionate, devotion

She is my smile, pleasure, inspiration

She is my smile foundation, miracle, motivation

She is more than super hero

She is more than a best friend

She tolerates all my mistakes

She always gives me on new inspiration when I got demotivated

She always cares me like a new-born baby

I don't have any words to express her

She is not anyone else, she is my mother.

She is not just a mother, she is universe.

(By Josmina Begum)

7. Feminism

I looked upon the life
There were lows and highs
In between I found trapped in ties
It is dream to fly in the sky.
It's just life not without men
But a person who respect every human
Delivering girl is not sin nor profane
But parity of rights of male and female.
Upliftment is about updated thoughts and opportunity
availed
It's not the race of proving one's gender great
Feminism is misused by some female acting insane
There are thousand stories male suffering, domestic violence
It's high time we understand the meaning of equivalence
Feminism is all about equality of male and female.
(By Tauhida Tamanna)

8. Wings To Fly

I have my wings to fly, don't cut them, please.
Pardon me, you wouldn't because you care for me.
But then you would just not let me fly!
Why? Why?
Apprehensive of people around us?
I understand it a big fuss.
But first and foremost, it's the two of us
This is how I keep it up.
Remember, you loved me because I was happily flying,
And now when i don't, you complain me of dying,
Each day a little.... yes, I am dying,
Because I need my wings to fly.
You love me, I know
And I rely on you, you must know.
Not to decide my own nights.
But stand by me in my small fights.
Pray for me when I fly,
Be with me when I go a little higher.
I need to see confidence for me in your face
When I touch those vast skies.
Who might not fall, why are you scared?
Vulnerable, we all are here
I need my wings to fly

Fly, high and high!
(By Moksima Zaman)

9. It's a Girl

It's a girl!
Sight!
And that since day one, she's already had everything
She needs within herself
It's the world that convinced her she didn't
She was Ten, it was just a member,
Armed with broken experience episode of
Overpowering sorrow
The burdens of her past were shouldered by the
Weakness in her knees.
Her little eyes want to flash out her disturbing
Childhood
and eyes that would better belong on the face
of a much older woman
Someone came and heal her and broke her
and made her realize again, that world is malicious
She wishes someone had warned her
when she was younger
Now she stays up all night and weeps;
The ghosts of everything she has loved and lost.
Come back to haunt her in her sleep.
After a thousand versions of her she has shed a
thousands of skins to become the person she is today

She looked in the mirror,
And her soul speaks
If you ever feel overwhelmed by many people you once were,
remember,
Your bones have grown, but what makes them
has never changed.
(By Fahima Fakharuddin)

10. Freedom

I want to decide,
I want to go outside,
I want to give suggestion,
But I am stopped.
I want to learn,
I want to earn.
But I am disallowed.
I am neither black nor white
I am an Indian Brown
I am ignored, hated
As I want to do according to my own.
Feeling the family is utmost important
They tell me to cook,
But who can understand them
That I like to read books.
Believe me, I am not a criminal
I never committed any crime,
But I am a woman
Who is deprived of everything
Everything!
(By Sumaiya Kalam)

11. The Light

Almost the darkness and desire,

Would you once care to be the light?

Absorbing all the dimmed thoughts

Would you once

Brighten up the sphere?

Those lost souls

The misguided wanderers

The once lost of cause

Would you be the light?

That shows them the way?

Be the light once

Being smiles.

Guide once.

Restore faith

Lead miles

And darkness well,

It has to pass.

Be the light in someone's life

Cherish the bright moments

Feel the bright thoughts

And for once be the glimmer

Be the hope

Be the light!

EDITOR: ADITI GHOSH

(By Reema Ingtipi)

12. Soothing

Meeting again, making new old memory.
Fragrance of you my life, customed with smile;
Moment spent of us with delight
Your introvert Ness finding comfort in me.
Hustle - bustle of cryptic world is vain, in your innocent
talks;
Everlasting conversations of life's pessimistic moment
And turning it to be the best one,
I, the first one for you and likewise you
Never bed up of selecting attires,
Will always wait for the next meet, again
(By Sima Devi)

13. Nature through my Eyes

I want to show you nature
Through my eyes, nature
which gives me pleasure
And soothes my eyes.
The blue sky, the following river
The singing birds, the shining stars
All encourage me to learn more
And to learn from mistakes
When I notice the beauty of mountains,
Trees, sunrise and sunset
And take a look at the dancing leaves,
My mind dances in glee
Like a happy dancing bee.
(By Momtaj Begum)

14. Story of my Life in Ten Lines

Born to the best mom on this beautiful earth.
I was little luckier than the rest.
Simply successful school life
Followed by flourishing fun at college
Getting married to my mate from childhood
Filled my life with love and merriment.
Working as a teacher who is favourite of all
Mother to two daughters who are now too small
My story seems like a joyride.
But trust me, it was full of jolts and jerks
(By Hasina Sultana Tapadar)

15. Journey of Recognition

I, who's never been recognized,
Searching for my recognition,
My recognition lies within you.
You! Whose journey has started since time Immortal.
And is still a journey,
Journey of recognition.
Will it ever meet its end?
And it will, what will be its end?
I am proud of the woman,
I am today because
I went through hell of time
To become her.
(By Javeen Akhtar)

16. Still, I rise

You may write me down in history
With your bitter, twisted lies.
You may tread me in the very dirt
But still, like dust, I'll rise.
Does my sassiness upset you?
Why are you beset with gloom?
Cause I walk I have got oil wells
Pumping in my living room.
Just like moons and like suns,
With the certainly of tides,
Just like hope springing high,
Still, I'll rise.
(By Wasima Yasmin)

17. An Unruly Rain

All over rainy here
Nothing to fear,
When it was the time of being frosted
You did vanish like a frustrated
But even than something was caring
That is very rearing.
It is very painful when something frustrated
But I am still obsessed from all that,
Knowing that you are acute formal.
But it is a dilemma to call
What is all around my mind.
Don't pretend again to be kind
That doesn't it is love
Because you are like a viral cough
Still a n unstoppable rain here
That's all that is lovely here.

(By Begum Sitara Islam)

18. Our Life

Life can be the sunshine
One peaceful day with bright blue sky.
Our life can be the raindrops
That fall like tears squeezed from our eyes,
Life can be the heaven,
That we'll only reach through hell.
Since we won't know that we are happy,
If we have not been sad as well.
Life can teach hard lessons,
But we'll be wiser once we know,
That even roses both sunshine,
And a touch of rain to grow.
(By Mubashira Khatun)

www.ingramcontent.com/pod-product-compliance
Lightning Source LLC
Chambersburg PA
CBHW031649170726
47990CB00019B/3095